Published by Creative Education
P.O. Box 227, Mankato, Minnesota 56002
Creative Education is an imprint of
The Creative Company
www.thecreativecompany.us

Design and production by The Design Lab
Art direction by Rita Marshall
Printed by Corporate Graphics in the
United States of America

Photographs by Alamy (Alaska Stock LLC), Dreams-
time (Cumulus, Twildlife), Getty Images (Blue and
White, John Eastcott and Yva Momatiuk), iStockphoto
(Andrey Artykov, Roman Krochuk, Rich Legg, Philip
Puleo, Eliza Snow, Paul Tessier)

Library of Congress Cataloging-in-Publication Data
Riggs, Kate.
Moose / by Kate Riggs.
p. cm. — (Amazing animals)
Summary: A basic exploration of the appearance,
behavior, and habitat of moose, Earth's largest deer.
Also included is a story from folklore explaining how
moose interact with other animals.
Includes bibliographical references and index.
ISBN 978-1-60818-111-7
1. Moose—Juvenile literature. I. Title. II. Series.
QL737.U55R54 2012
599.65'7—dc22   2010049131

CPSIA: 030111 PO1446

First Edition
9 8 7 6 5 4 3 2 1

AMAZING ANIMALS

MOOSE

BY KATE RIGGS

CREATIVE EDUCATION

Moose are about twice as big as the second-largest deer, elk

The moose is the biggest deer in the world. There are six kinds of moose. They are named for their habitats. Most moose live on the continent of North America.

continent one of Earth's seven big pieces of land

habitats places where animals live

Moose have thick fur to keep them warm. The fur is light or dark brown in color. Male moose have antlers on top of their heads. A pair of antlers on an older moose can be more than six feet (1.8 m) across!

The pair of antlers on a male moose is called a rack

The largest moose is the Yukon-Alaska moose. It can be more than seven feet (2.1 m) tall at the shoulder. A male Yukon-Alaska moose can weigh as much as 1,400 pounds (635 kg).

Yukon-Alaska moose live in the coldest habitats of all moose

*Moose can dive underwater
and like to swim*

Moose live in forests. They like to be near water, such as a stream or lake. Moose have to watch out for **predators**. Wolves and bears sometimes attack moose.

predators animals that kill and eat other animals

A moose eats plants from the water and from land. It likes to eat leaves from willow, birch, and aspen trees. A moose will eat twigs and bark if there are no leaves on the trees.

The way that moose eat plants is called browsing

Calves weigh about 30 pounds (14 kg) at birth

A mother moose has one or two **calves** at a time. The calves drink milk from their mother. When they are two weeks old, calves start eating plants, too. A one-year-old calf leaves its mother and finds its own home. Wild moose can live for about 20 years.

calves baby moose

Most moose live alone. They stay in an area called a home range. Sometimes moose leave their home range to go somewhere else for the winter. Then they live in groups to stay warm and safe.

Wyoming moose leave hilly homes to find plants in winter

A moose uses its teeth
to grind up twigs

Moose spend a lot of time eating. They need to eat 45 to 60 pounds (20–27 kg) of plants each day. Moose have a special stomach with four sections. This helps them **digest** all the plants.

digest to break down food in the stomach

People can see a lot of wild moose in Canada and Alaska. Sometimes, moose live close to towns and can be seen walking down the street. It is exciting to see these huge deer in town and in their forest habitats!

People in cars have to watch out for moose

A Moose Story

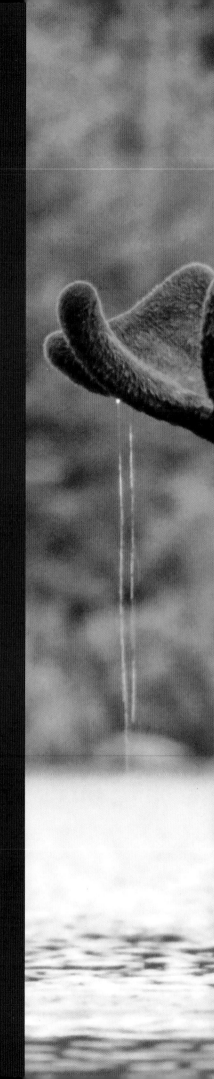

How do moose get along with other animals? American Indians used to tell a story about this. Once, a moose was standing in a stream eating plants. The catfish who lived there did not want Moose to eat their plants. They attacked Moose's feet with their sharp, pointy fins, and Moose stomped on their heads when he tried to get out of the water. To this day, catfish have flat heads because they did not want to share.

Read More

Snedden, Robert. *Northern Forests*. North Mankato, Minn.: Smart Apple Media, 2005.

Wrobel, Scott. *Moose*. North Mankato, Minn.: Smart Apple Media, 2001.

Web Sites

Mooseworld for Kids
http://www.mooseworld.com/forkids.htm
This site has games about moose to play.

TLC Family: Moose Activities
http://tlc.howstuffworks.com/family/moose-activities2.htm
This site has instructions on how to make your own moose antlers.